Arboreal

CORINNA BOARD

Black Cat Poetry Press

Editor: Satya Bosman
Artist Design: Lucia Bosman
www.blackcatpress.co.uk

Cover art design by Lucia Bosman
ISBN: 978-1-7397811-6-3

Contents

This is not a poem

It's a forest.

There are wild things here:
listen to the words howl,

the hoot of the vowels,
blinking their saucer eyes,

the peckpeckpeck of consonants,
lines scuttling across the page,

commas digging their claws in,
ampersands twisting like ivy.

It smells of pine & lichen & rot.
Close your eyes & take a whiff.

Genesis

In the beginning,
there was a seed: embryonic,
coiled in darkness, a tiny eye –
new-born blind.

You sleep.
You dream.
You wait.

Suddenly, an ache; a slow
splitting from crown to foot,
as something cracks
then breaks
open.

A spidering of roots,
a shoot unwinds;
charmed snake,
reaching up.

Sun-starved fledgling,
leaves feathering,
defenceless.

I hope you know
I'm rooting for you.

Little green Icarus –
if you fall,
I fall.

Embla

I am Embla,
first of my kind, last of my kind,
born from bark and the whim of a god.

My mother, the sea, shaped me to please
the man whose breath brought me to life.

Some say my name means Elm,
and it's true that, like the world tree,
my roots dig deep,

but no dragon curls at my feet,
no god hangs from my gallow-boughs.

Yggdrasil, I envy you,
how does it feel to carry the cosmos in your arms?

Each world an apple ripe with promise,
tainted by original sin,
roots cradling the depths of Hel.

I envy your longevity:
one day I will return to dust;
my life another ring on your trunk.

I am Embla,
first of my kind, first of many;
mother to humanity,

a woman who dreamt she was a tree.

Old man in the woods

Let me tell you the story
of the old man in the woods:

tree-hugger, leaf-muncher,
bird-whisperer.

Too many names (I've forgotten half of them).
Someone who's spent so long in the wild
they've become it:
a fusion of human and tree.
If you'd seen him –
skin like bark, moss-caked eye,
you'd believe me.
When our nan used to say:

Stay out of those woods
or you'll end up like him!

I didn't listen, then I grew roots –
for a minute or two I couldn't move.
I know what you're thinking:

There are far worse things that could
happen to someone than becoming a tree.

I agree, to a certain extent.
That man knows things,
he's soaked up secrets through his taproot.

Wise old oak.

Lullaby

There are no wolves here.
Cuckoo-pint, fungi, lichen;
some of which might possibly kill you
if you popped one into your tiny mouth,
but no wolves.
Rickety oaks, beeches, hawthorn,
cushions of moss – so soft, so green.
You could lie down and rest. Why don't you?
Under the canopy it's surprisingly warm;
the rooks will sing you to sleep.
In the woods of the mind
every shadow has teeth,
but there are no wolves.
Not even one.

Portable forest

after Roger Robinson

Picture a miniature forest –
like a snow globe with trees.

An ecosystem reproduced:
birch, oak, flutter of aspen,

beeches forming a cathedral;
spindle fingers stretched in prayer,

dogwood cowering in the understory,
bluebells, bowing their heads,

pretending not to know they're beautiful.
Surprise of wild garlic,

stink of moss and mulch;
carrying that around in your coat pocket

as a cure for the winter blues,
rolling the perfect marble of it

in your hand like a fidget toy,
staining your fingers with sap.

Heartwood

I want to disappear into those hills;
pack my heart in a bag and go.

I'll leave in the quiet hours,
when the dew polishes the grass

to a shine, when the sun hides
and the moon rolls her ghost-wheel

across the sky. I've set my sights
on the line of trees poking over the curve;

a stegosaurus spine of cedars and firs.
I'll make a home in their greenness:

the long breath of it, chlorophyll
sweetness, all I'll ever need.

Mycena Haematopus

Do I have to be an expert in fungi to write about you?
Mycologist says Google. *Mycology* [Mai. ko. luh. jee].
I mouth each syllable as if trying to learn your language.
When I was small, someone must have told me
to stamp on toadstools because they were bad:
I remember the devastation of flesh under boot,
the guilt I felt for destroying something so fragile.
I read that you ooze a wine-red fluid when crushed
or cut. It doesn't say if you are poisonous,
but look how beautiful you are in your conical hats:
thin-stemmed jungle, arrowing upwards,
a bioluminescent bloom of jellyfish,
fruiting bodies pink-tinged, curved like cervixes.
Fitting, then, that your Latin name means *bleeding*.

Unpopular opinion

Autumn is a monster.

In October, she's downright murderous:
throttling the green out of trees
until they tear their leaves out in grief,
steamrolling through forests and parks,
leaving a trail of bloody roadkill:
berries' shrivelled hearts, eviscerated conkers,
acorn skulls smashed to a pulp,
pine cones left to rot in stinking puddles.
No wonder the squirrels can't sit still –
given half the chance, she'd make
a fur coat from their pelts to keep warm
in December. That's when she grows weak;
slinks like a fox through hungry streets.
Come solstice, she's a wreck – I can't help
pitying her; she'll be dead by morning.

Silver birches

You always look best at night,
huddled in the darkness like a coven,

when the moon perches in your branches
and paints you shades of alabaster.

I run my hand over trunks riddled
with scars; even you are vulnerable.

Old bark peels into curls that fall
like rolled cigarettes or shed skin.

I smooth a piece between my fingers
until the surface cracks. I don't know

what I expect to find: a protection spell,
an invitation scrawled in sap: *Join us*.

In the park

Trees form a shield
between the park and the road,
but the dull howl arrows my senses;
opening the wound of loneliness.

I sit here bleeding:
people and dogs float by.
Only the moon sees me
with her half an eye;
safe in her cloud nest.

This is the city, after all,
where sorrow hides in plain sight,
and a heart can be buried
at the roots of an oak
and left there for winter.

Field song

Birdsong's ricochet: robin, hedge sparrow.
You measure the silence in between notes,

still don't know how to name each bird,
move on through fields where oilseed rape

spills its blooms in buttery curls
that erupt into dust thick with pollen.

To your left, the Evenlode snakes its way south,
skylarks tease the air into ribbons of sound.

You reach the woods, step carefully over
primroses, constellations of anemones,

to sit on the trunk of a fallen oak.
Lichen writes its braille on bark,

a blackbird pours its song into the quiet.
You pick up your thoughts, trace the curve

of the bridleway round to the lake
draped with willows and Canada geese.

It's getting late – the dark calls you home.

Portrait of the lake at sunrise

The willow leans down, pulls dawn
from the water: glistening new-born,
slick as a fish.

The sun is just beginning to rise;
pouring her fire into the lake.

An early mallard swims into the flames,
emerging unscathed. A pair of herons sit

by the shore, scanning the surface – two
charred ghosts on the brink of morning.

Water ripples and pools in circles;
shattering the perfect mirror of trees.

The branches of an oak shimmer
in the inferno, but do not burn.

I've been trying to write this poem for weeks

It begins with an old man walking down the drive towards a farm.
It begins with my grandfather.
It begins.

I am a child.
I am younger than seven years old.
I know this because I still live at my grandparents' house.
I know this because I'm happy.

This poem begins when my grandfather shuts the back door,
and walks down the drive in the half-light of morning.

The memory is so old now, I don't know if it's real or a dream.
I hope it's real.
I hope I can finish this poem.

My grandfather, in his tweed cap and blue overalls
tied at the waist with a piece of string.

I'm watching from the kitchen window,
I can't remember why I'm up this early;
it must be five-thirty or thereabouts.
I know I want to run after him,
but it's early and I'm not dressed.

I stand at the kitchen window;
at the threshold between possibility and regret,
but I don't go.

He crosses the old rickyard,
turns left towards the gate into the big field,
slides the rusty lock, climbs over the fence.

A little girl stands alone in a kitchen,
unaware this moment will become a ghost
that haunts her often.

She stares at the door, then goes back to bed.

Time traveller

Today, I time travel.

I walk through the door
and decide I'm eighteen again.

Is it as easy as it sounds?
I'd like to say yes,
but you'd know I was lying.

Here I am,
in a field where I used to dream.

I sit cross-legged
on the lumpy ground and pretend
it's comfortable.

Memories gather in wisps
then scatter when I touch them.

A familiar taste teases my tongue –
I could call it regret, but that would mean
I fucked up.

I am eighteen
If I repeat it enough, does that make it real?

I stare at the field, waiting for answers to grow –
it seems I've only planted questions.

The shed

Greasy windows that kept / the darkness in / feathers erupted
from a bucket / onto the floor / a smell I couldn't name / a noose
of baling twine / hung from the ceiling / like an unanswered ques-
tion / I was still small / didn't know what it meant / but looking
back / death was everywhere / pigs fattening in their pens / the
pet lambs that disappeared / the games we played / an obstacle
course / of deadly machinery / slurry's unforgiving quicksand /
my grandmother / pulling the guts from a chicken / the sudden
pearl / of an unlaid egg / I cried for days / when I found out /
that everything dies / the shed / its carpet of feathers / answering
a question / I never asked.

Elegy

'May you see her in the light-streaked skies and the company of trees. May you hear her in birdsong and down by the sea' Tess Ward.

You are not in the sky,
unless that cloud is your white hair.

The sky looks just the same as it did
yesterday. Swifts shriek and loop.

I read somewhere people used to call
them devil birds. That is why I struggle

with religion. If this wild screeching joy
is the afterlife, I'll take it. And the trees?

We scattered your ashes under the plum tree.
When my aunty sold the house, the new owners

chopped it down. Ashes to earth to roots.
I like to think they burned the wood

and you became ash again. A whorl
of smoke – up, up, up with the swifts.

Yes, there you are. I can finally see you.

The yew trees

They are everywhere.
Branches pointing upwards, as if to say:

Look.
This is where it ends,
this is where you're headed,

mimicking the stone angel on one
of the graves, with its graffiti of lichen.

The yews carry the cycle of life in their roots,
know what's waiting behind death's curtain.
They have been there
and survived.

I walk around for a while, not afraid;
a sense of peace emanates from the soil;
its tombs with names effaced by moss
and centuries, the stench of loss sweetened
by snowdrops growing on the uneven mounds.

I feel them watching me the whole time,
as if they know I want to believe but can't.
When I leave, I hear them whisper:
One day.

Chopped

A stump in this city of high-rise trees;
guillotined and left to rot.

Impossible to tell what you once were;
a wooden heart turned dark with mould,
your remains returned to the earth
so slowly.

Moss paints a map over exposed rings;
a green planet; clumps like continents,
an epitaph that reads:
life goes on.

Your lifeblood feeds the soil;
each drop a legacy,
a reminder that this isn't the end.

Jardin des plantes

She mops her face with a leaf of tissue
fished from the pocket of her *tailleur*,

adjusts the helmet of bobbed hair
with Chanel nails, fingers magpied in gold.

Twice a year, she roasts on the Côte D'Azur –
she likes to enjoy the good things in life,

everything else stays out of sight, out of mind.
She wanders through the *Serre des forêts tropicales*,

awkward traveller on this ark of biodiversity:
she's wearing the wrong shoes, the fabric

of her suit chafes her neck, her *brushing*
has started to look like a jungle fern.

She doesn't know why she's come here, but
she feels humbled by this wildness – she wants

to lie under the banana tree, let insects and spiders
crawl over her body, she wants to beg for forgiveness.

Though my mother-in-law does none of these things,
she's not quite the same when she leaves.

The bud of her heart has begun to open ever-so-slowly,
like the velvet-petalled orchid in the *Grande Serre*.

The woman outside my window

She's been here all night –
waiting, watching.
Still as a tree,
quiet as the space between breaths.

I swear she hasn't blinked.
I don't know what she wants and
I'm starting to wonder if she'll ever leave.

She could be smiling, it's hard to tell.
Her eyes are dark as rooks
and the sun has forgotten to rise
even though it's nine a.m.

Did I mention the bird?
Feathered flame, perched in her hair,
setting the morning on fire with its song.

I know she'll still be there when I'm gone;
eyes like windows,
little mirrors full of ash.

Eve

after 'The Temptation of Eve' by Walter Crane

In the picture,
you're bound to the apple tree:
serpent-coiled, prisoner of fate.

There can be no other ending, it's too late.
The fruit unbitten sits like a grenade
in your palm; perfectly ripe, weighted.

There's something disturbing about it—
how the artist must have explored
each curve

while you stood there,
unable to meet his gaze. Legs crossed,
arms splayed, as if crucified.

Animals are still gathering at your feet,
but the ark of your body bolts its doors,
floats for awhile, then slowly catches fire.

When I tell you I've been thinking about death

what I mean is: bury me
in a ship like a Viking,

I want to be close to the earth,
become food for worms.

I'm not trying to be morbid
just to give something back.

Did you know that
the Celts believed

in reincarnation, thought
their dead could return

as animals or plants?
Cover me in stones,

shroud me in the wisdom
of rock. Let the rain water

my bones and I'll grow into
a blackthorn tree. Burn

my body, throw my ashes
to the wind – dust to dust –

a murmuration of starlings
flying south for winter.

Of a feather

after Liz Berry

They'd been calling for days,
it was inevitable.
Out of the window I flew,
swapping skin for feathers.
Smaller and smaller
until I was light as air
and the flock claimed me.
I forgot everything I knew:
my children, the morning
commute, all the worries
that clipped my wings
and weighed me down.
I can't begin to describe it –
I was ash, I was ink, I was smoke.
It was like we'd stolen the sky,
and the sky kept trying to steal itself back.

Why I'm not afraid of the dark

A sound like thunder
pulls me to the window.

Someone has shot the sky;
a reddish glow bleeds

over the brook. Another boom
sends a flock of roosting starlings

into the air like shrapnel.
A firework fizzes up behind

the trees and bursts into ribbons.
Just fireworks...

Back inside, I unzip the cold
and exhale adrenaline.

I used to love them –
how they could turn the

night into a Picasso;
spattering it in gaudy paint.

Now I crave the darkness;
the silence that falls when

the canvas drains of colour,
and all that's left is the moon.

Boreal

for Ben Rawlence

The last forest will be boreal:
one final ring in the earth's trunk,
a pheromone scream, a swansong
ringing out above the permafrost.

The last tide will be boreal:
a crashing wave of conifers,
root to root with poplar, rowan, birch,
laying down wooden swords.

The last breath will be boreal:
a giant lung, parting gift of oxygen,
a stop-motion filmed over centuries;
played back until trees fall like dominoes.

Winter sun

We are playing hide and seek
and you're winning:

now I see you
                    now I don't

Suddenly
it's game-over

you're in my face
so bright I can't look

you sit on the brim of the horizon
worshipped by a congregation of trees:

We have sacrificed our leaves
now give us light,

let the chlorophyll be plentiful
next year

I wonder if they sense the change
in their roots

if they worry this could be the last winter
if they'll miss the cold when it's gone.

The last tree

for Seán Hewitt

Today the last tree died

Where there was birdsong,
only quiet remains:
blackbird's complaint,
trill of the wren,
rook's guttural caw.
Gone.

Today the last tree died

The air hangs heavy all around.
No insects or spiders
scuttling over bark,
no fallen leaves to mark
the changing seasons,
just emptiness.

Today the last tree died

Generations of memories
locked in its heartwood.
All we have left
are reasons to grieve.

Matryoshka

She feels at home
in her wooden cocoon:
lipstick smile, pink moon cheeks,
they'll never guess what's hidden
under all that paint.
No one bothers to look
beyond the veneer.
If they did, they'd hear
the tick-tick-tick of her linden heart
beating out the years like a tiny drum,
like a tiny bomb;
painted roses still have thorns.
When it's her turn to be reborn,
she'll rise from the bodies
of her sister-selves
as they fall, cracked shells,
at her tiny feet.

Arboreal

I've made it
to the heartwood;
this is my home now.

Nothing can hurt me here:
fortress of bark,
amniotic sap.

I've waited
my whole life
for such belonging:

let me breathe
through your lungs
and feel what you feel,

hold the earth's
beating heart
in my roots.

Acknowledgements

Some of the poems in this pamphlet, sometimes in different versions, were first published in the following journals:

Anthropocene: *Portrait of the Lake at Sunrise, In the Park*

Atrium: *Mycena Haematopus*

Green Ink Poetry: *Genesis*

Spelt: *I've Been Trying to Write this Poem for Weeks*

Wild Roof Journal: *Embla*

The Yew Trees was longlisted for the inaugural Rosemary McLeish Poetry Prize, judged by Jane Burn, and subsequently appeared in an anthology published by Wordsmithery.

Many of these poems were seeded in a wonderful workshop 'In praise of trees' led by Seán Hewitt.

www.blackcatpress.co.uk